Surf and Turf
Mar y Tierra

Cookbook
Nydia Sagre

Copyright © 2023 Nydia Sagre, All rights reserved.

No part of this publication may be reproduced, stored in a retrieval system or transmitted in any form or by any means, electronic, mechanical, photocopying, recording or otherwise, without prior permission of Halo Publishing International.

The views and opinions expressed in this book are those of the author and do not necessarily reflect the official policy or position of Halo Publishing International. Any content provided by our authors are of their opinion and are not intended to malign any religion, ethnic group, club, organization, company, individual or anyone or anything.

For permission requests, write to the publisher, addressed "Attention: Permissions Coordinator," at the address below.

Halo Publishing International
7550 WIH-10 #800, PMB 2069,
San Antonio, TX 78229

First Edition, November 2023
ISBN: 978-1-63765-525-2

The information contained within this book is strictly for informational purposes. Unless otherwise indicated, all the names, characters, businesses, places, events and incidents in this book are either the product of the author's imagination or used in a fictitious manner. Any resemblance to actual persons, living or dead, or actual events is purely coincidental.

Halo Publishing International is a self-publishing company that publishes adult fiction and non-fiction, children's literature, self-help, spiritual, and faith-based books. We continually strive to help authors reach their publishing goals and provide many different services that help them do so. We do not publish books that are deemed to be politically, religiously, or socially disrespectful, or books that are sexually provocative, including erotica. Halo reserves the right to refuse publication of any manuscript if it is deemed not to be in line with our principles. Do you have a book idea you would like us to consider publishing? Please visit www.halopublishing.com for more information.

I dedicate this book to my grandchildren, Ethan, Olivia, Nathan, Katie, and Carol.

Contents

Surf — 9

Arroz con Calamares (Squid) — 11
Shrimp Scampi — 13
Enchilado de Camarones/Langosta — 15
Garlic Spicy Shrimp and Lobster Tail — 17
Creamy Garlic Shrimp — 20

Turf — 21

Nydia Prime Rib — 23
Au Jus — 24
Nydia Whole Filete Mignon in Oven — 27
Nydia's Individual Filet Mignon — 30
Albondigas Cuban Meatballs — 32

Meatloaf	35
Picadillo with Salsa and Diced Tomatoes	37
Cuban Fritas	39
Chopped Beef	41

This is what I mean in my recipes when I write

Sazones

4 sazones

- Sazon Completa
- Garlic Powder
- Ground Cumin
- Oregano

3 sazones

- Sazone Completa
- Garlic Powder
- Ground Cumin

2 sazones

- Sazone Completa
- Garlic Powder

Cubitos de pollo are

Chicken Bouillon

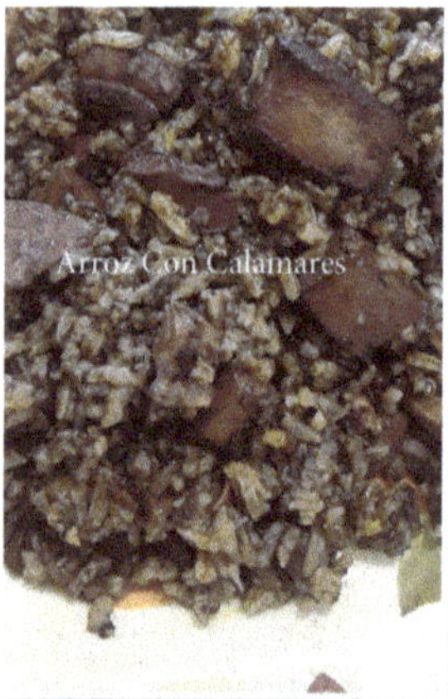
Arroz Con Calamares

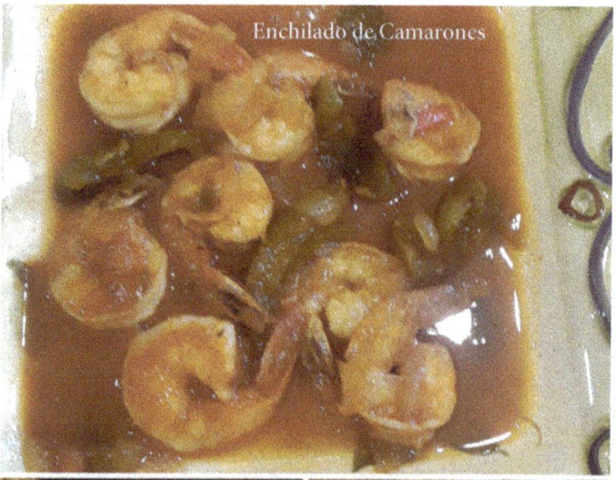
Enchilado de Camarones

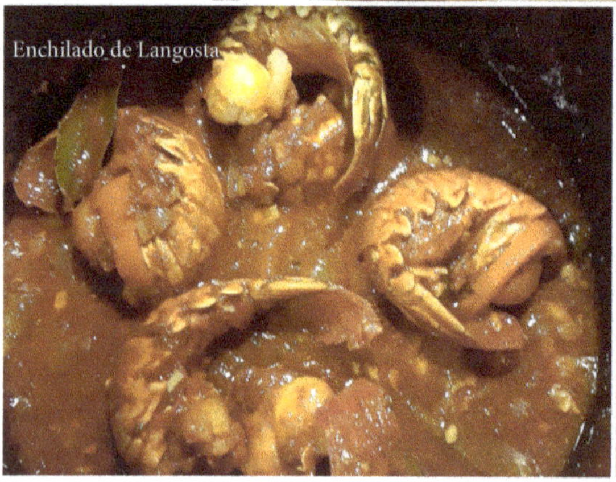
Enchilado de Langosta

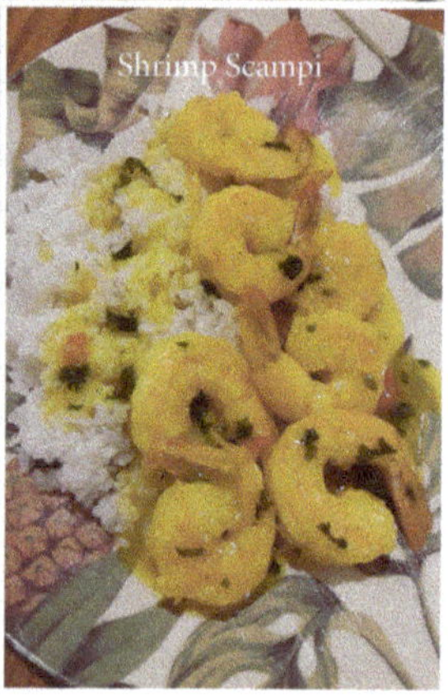
Shrimp Scampi

Arroz con Calamares (Squid)

- 5 cans 4 oz. squid filete in their own ink
- 1 small onion diced
- 2 cup of white rice
- ¼ green pepper cut small
- Salt 1 teaspoon
- ½ cup of vino seco
- 2½ cups of water
- 3 sazones
- Olive oil
- 1 cubito de pollo
- 4 garlic cloves minced

Add olive oil to bottom of a quart pot, sauté green pepper a few minutes, and then add onions, sauté a few minutes add garlic sauté a few minutes.

Add 4 cans of squid with its ink; the 5th can, only add the filets not the ink. Add rice, Vino Seco and sazones, cook for a minute.

Add water, and salt, bring to boil, cover pot and reduce heat to low #1 cook for 25 minutes. When done mix rice with fork and let sit for 10 minutes before serving.

Surf and Turf Mar y Tierrra

Shrimp Scampi

Ingredient

- 2 lbs. peeled and deveined Shrimp
- Parmesan cheese
- 8 garlic cloves minced
- Olive oil
- ¼ cup vino seco
- Juice of 1 lemon
- ¼ cup heavy cream (optional)
- 2 Tablespoons butter

Olive oil to bottom of large frying pan, Sauté shrimp on high for a few minutes on each side then remove from pan. Lower heat and add

Vino Seco, lemon juice, and butter. Cook a few minutes and then add garlic, cook for ½ minutes, then return shrimp to pan. Optional if you want to make with an Alfredo white sauce, when you return shrimp to pan add cream and sprinkle some parmesan cheese, cook a few minutes, don't let cream boil. Turn off heat. You can also make with an Oriental Sauce.

Enchilado de Camarones/ Langosta

- 2 lbs. shrimp cleaned and deveined
- 1 bay leaf
- 1 head of garlic, cloves diced
- 2 cans of tomato sauce
- 2 cups vino seco
- ¼ green, red, orange, yellow bell peppers cut into small pieces
- 2 tablespoons worcestershire
- 4 sazones
- 1 tablespoon cilantro minced
- Olive oil
- 2 medium onions chopped

Olive oil to pot, sauté shrimp and then remove from pot, you will add later. Sauté peppers, then add 1 onion sauté, then add ½ of the garlic sauté for ½ min. then lower temperature to medium.

Add tomato sauce, sazones, Worcestershire, bay leaf and cook for a few minutes. Then add vino seco, other onion and remaining garlic. Simmer for 10 minutes then add shrimp and cilantro, simmer for 5 minutes and turn off heat. Allow to rest for an hour before serving.

You can also substitute with Lobster.

Garlic Spicy Shrimp and Lobster Tail

- Florida Lobster tail
- Garlic cloves minced
- Butter 1 stick
- Olive oil to pan
- Parsley
- 4 sazones

I use frozen lobster tails, because they are quick frozen when caught. Place them in cold water for 1 hour to thaw.

After, cook on medium heat for half an hour. Then bring to a rapid boil for another 15 minutes, until lobster tails curl up in a ball.

Melt a stick of butter, then add 8 cloves of minced garlic.

You can also add sautéed shrimp. Serve with rice or toasted bread.

Surf and Turf Mar y Tierrra

Creamy Garlic Shrimp

- 16 Large Shrimp
- 1 cup heavy cream
- 10 garlic cloves minced olive oil
- Flour lightly to shrimp
- 2 Tablespoon vino seco juice from 1/2 a lime

Dry shrimp with paper towel, then place in flour. Heat oil to bottom of pot, add floured shrimp, cook a few minutes turning once then add garlic and cook for a minute add lemon and vino seco. Add cream and bring it to a soft boil for 2 minutes so sauce can thicken. Serve with fettuccine or rice.

Nydia Prime Rib

- 6 lb Black Angus Beef Loin Boneless Buy at Argentinean Restaurant or Butcher for good grade of meat
- 2 Tablespoons of Olive Oil
- 5 Teaspoon full McCormick Grill mates Montreal Seasoning

Pre heat oven to 450 Bake.

Mix oil and Montreal Seasoning and let sit in bowl for 5 minutes.

Make a few cuts into the Fatty side of Loin, but not into the meat.

Apply rub on Fatty side only. Leave it out for one hour to reach close to room temperature before cooking.

Place Loin, fatty side up in a Roasting pan, so loin doesn't sit on drippings.

Put in oven for 15 minutes at 450, then reduce temp to 300 to 325 until middle of loin reaches desired temp. Rare - 115, Medium Rare- 120, Medium – 130.

Do not baste at anytime, you don't want to ruin the crispiness of outer Loin.

Take out and let it sit for 15 minutes before you slice. Use this time to make Au Jus.

Au Jus

When you remove Loin from rack to cutting board. Add 1 cup of good red wine to dripping and scrape bottom of pan. Add a few shots of Worchshire.

Transfer dripping to a frying pan if you can't put pan directly on stove. Add 1 cup of Chicken Broth and 3 minced Garlic cloves, and half a small onion cut small, bring to boil and reduce sauce till it thickens.

Slice Rib Loin and serve. Add juice at table.

6 lb Rib Loin serves 5 adults.

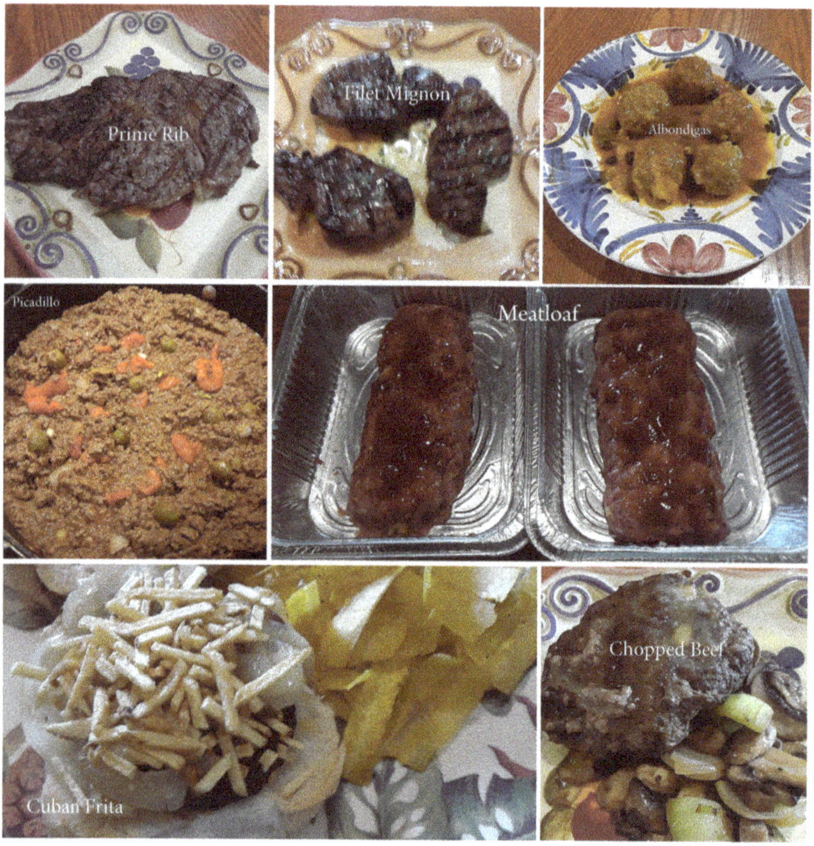
Prime Rib
Filet Mignon
Albondigas
Picadillo
Meatloaf
Cuban Frita
Chopped Beef

Nydia Whole Filete Mignon in Oven

- 6 lb. Black Angus whole Beef Tenderloin/Filete
- Buy at Argentinean Carneceria for good grade of meat
- Supermarkets and Costco/BJ don't sell Black Angus grade
- 3 tsp of Canola Oil, don't use Olive oil, because you will cook at high temp
- 1 full teaspoon of McCormick Grill mates Montreal Seasoning

Pre heat oven to 400 Bake.

Mix oil and Montreal Seasoning and let sit in bowl for 5 minutes.

Cut off both ends of Filete and use for another recipe, you want Filete in oven to be the same height.

Apply rub to top part of Filete and leave out for 1 hour. Meats should not be put in Oven cold, cause it ruins the tenderness of meat.

Place Filete in a Roasting pan , with highest part of Filete to back of oven.

Put in oven for 10 minutes at 400 then lower temp to 350 for about 30 minutes till you reach a 135 Temp with Meat probe to thickest part of Filete for Medium rare to center. If no one likes medium rare then cook till temp is 140 before you take out of oven.

Take out of oven and let sit for 10 minutes. Meat is still cooking, you must slice at this time to stop meat from cooking. If it is to rare for some people then put sliced pieces in oven till you see desired color.

Make Bearnaise sauce while Filete is in oven.

Put 1 Stick of Butter in a medium sauce pan, with two large egg yokes for half an hour in refrigerator before you start making sauce so both have same temperature.

Before you start cooking add 1 Tablespoon of Tarragon vinegar, 1 Tablespoon lemon juice, a palm size of salt and 1/2 teaspoon of dried tarragon.

Put sauce pan on cold stove top and put temperature on low. use a whisk and mix sauce turning in the same direction till Butter melts and sauce thickens.

Remove from heat when sauce thickens. Do not raise temperature when cooking or you will make scramble eggs.

Serve at table.

Nydia's Individual Filet Mignon

- 4 Filet Steaks 3 inches wide
- Salt
- McCormick Grill mates Montreal Seasoning
- Avocado oil
- 4 Garlic cloves minced
- 1 Sprig of Cilantro per steak
- 6 tablespoons Butter

Preheat Oven to 450 Bake

Take meat out of refrigerator 30 minutes before cooking, Mix 3 tablespoon oil with 1 tsp Montreal seasoning, let rest for 5 minutes before adding to meat.

Add salt to one side of meat, side you will sear first , then add rub/oil mix to both sides 30 minutes before you cook.

Heat a frying pan that can also go in Oven on high heat, when pan is hot, add oil to bottom of pan and immediately add steaks, do not touch steaks, sear for 3 minutes, then flip and sear for another 3 minutes Last minute of searing, add 1 tablespoon cut up butter per steak and cilantro. to pan. When 3 minutes have passes put pan in oven for 3 minutes.

Take out and add 2 tablespoons of butter to pan, move pan to mix, add garlic then baste top of each steak. Take steaks out of pan and plate to stop cooking process. Let sit for a few minutes before eating. Can add more of butter from pan on top of plated Filete.

You can use any herb you want. I used cilantro for hispanic taste.

Albondigas Cuban Meatballs

- 3.0 lbs. ground meat and ground pork meatloaf mix
- 2 cans tomato sauce
- Olive oil
- 2 cups vino seco
- 2 eggs beaten
- 1 large onion chopped medium
- 4 sazones
- ¼ of a medium sized red, green, yellow, and orange bell peppers, cut into medium size squares.
- Salt to meat
- 8 garlic cloves minced

3 slices of white bread, wet bread under running water and then squeeze water out of breads, add to meat. I prefer this to bread crumbs.

Place meat in a bowl, add salt. Then add beaten eggs and wet bread. Mix with a fork; do not completely break up the pieces of bread. They give space to the meatballs and allow the flavor to enter meat. I form meatballs with a large spoon.

Add Oil to bottom of a large pot, on medium high sauté peppers, then onions, then Garlic for ½ minute. Don't burn your garlic. Lower temp to medium #5, add tomato sauce, and sazones.

Cook a few minutes then add vino seco, continue to cook and then add meatballs. Bring liquid to a boil, cover pot and reduce heat to #5 medium setting. Cook covered for 25 minutes. When done remove from heat and add a box of raisins.

Since I rarely eat rice, I have substituted it with small carrots, which I add when I add onions.

You can add any vegetable of your choice. If you see that there is too much liquid, after cooking for 25 minutes, uncover pot and continue cooking another 5 minutes. Don't reduce all the sauce, that's the best part, it will thicken when it cools.

Meatloaf

- Meatloaf mixes with ground beef and pork about 1.5 lbs.
- 4 sazones
- 2 white breads wet in water and then squeeze water out
- 2 oz. chorizo molido
- 1 beaten egg
- Salt to meat

Mix all ingredients and form into 1 loaf. Rectangle shape, make ends square not round. Cover the top of loaves with topping, don't put on the sides. Bake uncovered at 350 for 40 minutes.

Topping:

- ⅓ cup of ketchup
- 1 tablespoons of sugar
- 1 tablespoon yellow mustard

Picadillo with Salsa and Diced Tomatoes

- 2.0 pounds of ground sirloin
- 1 large onion chopped
- 8 garlic cloves minced
- 10 olives
- 1 chunky salsa jar
- 2 cubitos de pollo
- 1 can 14.5 oz. diced tomatoes
- 4 sazones

Brown beef in a skillet until almost cooked. Add Olives, Onions, and 4 sazones. Cook a few minutes then add garlic, cook for a few minutes.

Lower temperature #4, add Salsa, cubitos de pollo, discard liquid from diced tomato can, and then add and simmer for 5 minutes and turn off heat.

You can use Mild, Medium or Hot Salsa. I use this for Nachos, Fajitas, or over any type of rice.

Cuban Fritas

- 1.5 pound of ground chuck
- ¼ pound of ground pork
- Salt
- ¼ pound ground chorizo
- Raw onions chopped small
- 1 tablespoon worcestershire
- Canola Oil
- 2 garlic cloves minced
- ¼ teaspoon ground cumin
- 1 teaspoon smoked paprika
- Hamburger buns

Mix all ingredients except Onions. Make into a round meatball.

Place oil to bottom of small frying pan. Add meatballs to pan and cook on medium #4. Rotate meatball until it is cooked on all sides, then flatten into a patty. Cook until done. Do not press down on patties or you will squeeze out the juices and flavor.

Optional, add small chopped small onions and the Cuban way is to fry shredded small pieces of potatoes and top on frita when serving or top with Shoe string potatoes.

Surf and Turf Mar y Tierrra

Chopped Beef

- 1.5 lbs. ground chuck beef
- 1 egg
- 2 slices white bread (soak in water under faucet, then squeeze water out) crumble in large chucks into meat
- 1 large onion chopped large
- Salt
- 1 stick of unsalted butter melted
- Worcestershire
- Sliced mushrooms (optional)

Bake 350 F.

Place meat in a bowl, and lightly salt. Add unbeaten egg, and wet bread. Add a few shots of Worcestershire. Mix and form into four oval patties.

Place in an oven proof pan. Pour melted butter over patties, and then add a few generous shots of Worcestershire over each patty. Place in Oven for 20 minutes, and then turn over patties. Add onions, mushrooms and cook another 15 minutes. If you want gravy then add a tablespoon of flour and mix when meat is done.

www.ingramcontent.com/pod-product-compliance
Lightning Source LLC
Chambersburg PA
CBHW040323050426
42453CB00017B/2440